BEHIND THE BRAND
AMAZON

BY RACHEL FIRST

BLASTOFF! DISCOVERY

BELLWETHER MEDIA • MINNEAPOLIS, MN

This is not an official Amazon book. It is not approved by or connected with Amazon.com, Inc.

This edition first published in 2025 by Bellwether Media, Inc.

No part of this publication may be reproduced in whole or in part without written permission of the publisher.
For information regarding permission, write to Bellwether Media, Inc., Attention: Permissions Department,
6012 Blue Circle Drive, Minnetonka, MN 55343.

Library of Congress Cataloging-in-Publication Data

LC record for Amazon available at: https://lccn.loc.gov/2024021920

Text copyright © 2025 by Bellwether Media, Inc. BLASTOFF! DISCOVERY and associated logos are trademarks and/or registered trademarks of Bellwether Media, Inc. Bellwether Media is a division of Chrysalis Education Group.

Editor: Betsy Rathburn   Series Designer: Andrea Schneider   Book Designer: Josh Brink

Printed in the United States of America, North Mankato, MN.

TABLE OF CONTENTS

ADD TO CART!	4
BECOMING #1	6
ALWAYS GROWING	18
HELPING OTHERS	26
A SPECIAL HOLIDAY	28
GLOSSARY	30
TO LEARN MORE	31
INDEX	32

ADD TO CART!

It is after school on a Friday. A new video game is out. Two sisters hope to buy it. They want to play it this weekend. They want to get snacks, too. The sisters ask their parents to help them.

Their parents realize that they need some things, too. They need dog food for the family pet. They also need a part to fix their car. They decide to order from the Amazon **app**. They log in on a smartphone. They add the items to their cart and pay. It will all be delivered tomorrow!

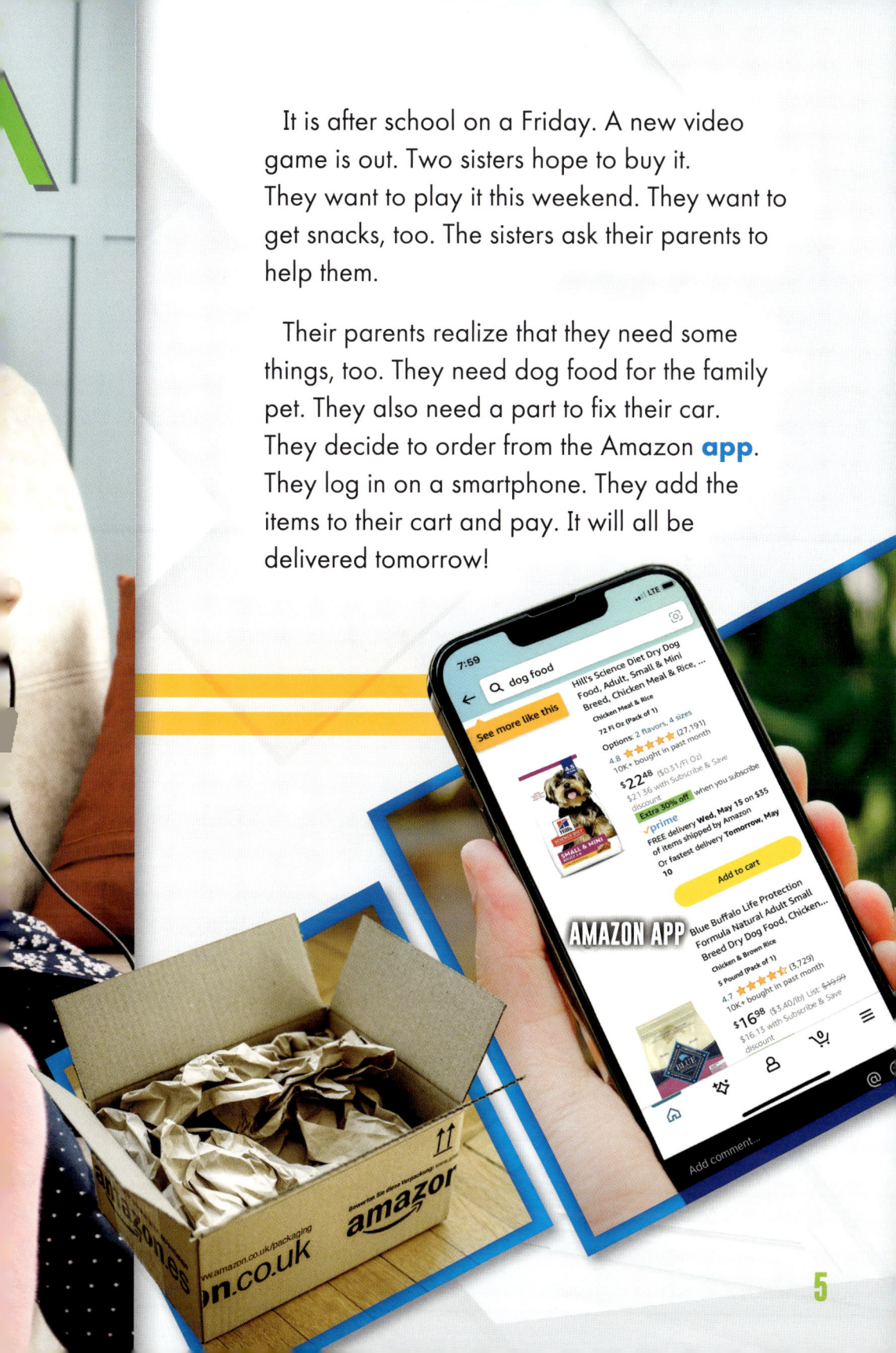

AMAZON APP

BECOMING #1

AMAZON GO STORE

AMAZON HEADQUARTERS
SEATTLE, WASHINGTON

Amazon is one of the world's largest **retailers**. Most of its sales are made online. Some cities have Amazon stores. Seattle, Washington, is home to the company's main **headquarters**. A second Amazon headquarters is in Arlington, Virginia.

People can buy almost anything on Amazon. Its **fulfillment centers** help people get orders quickly. Amazon's Prime Video brings entertainment to **subscribers**. Amazon Web Services (AWS) powers many websites. Amazon has its own products, too. The Kindle is for reading. The Echo is for music. Amazon also has many popular **subsidiaries**. These include Whole Foods Market and Twitch.

AMAZON HEADQUARTERS

SEATTLE, WASHINGTON

ARLINGTON, VIRGINIA

Amazon was started by Jeff Bezos in 1994. During this time, the internet was still new to many people. Jeff saw an opportunity. He decided to build an internet company. He wanted to sell something that would interest a lot of buyers. He decided to sell books.

JEFF BEZOS

BELLEVUE, WASHINGTON

AMAZON RIVER

The company started in Jeff's garage in Bellevue, Washington. He borrowed around $250,000 from his parents to start his company. He named it Amazon after the Amazon River, the world's widest river. Jeff wanted Amazon to have the world's widest selection of books!

GET BIG FAST

Jeff wanted Amazon to grow quickly. He made "Get Big Fast" a company saying. It was printed on employee shirts!

BOOKS IN AN AMAZON FULFILLMENT CENTER

Amazon grew quickly. By 1997, the company offered more than 2.5 million different books for sale.

ORIGINAL OWNERS

Amazon owned one-click ordering from 1999 to 2017. Since then, other websites can use the idea, too.

That same year, Amazon introduced one-click ordering. This solved a big problem that online retailers faced. Before then, buying online involved many clicks. Many shoppers filled their carts. But then they did not click to complete the purchase. This meant sellers did not get the sale. One-click ordering led to more sales for Amazon. By 1998, Amazon sales climbed to $610 million!

JEFF BEZOS

BORN January 12, 1964, in Albuquerque, New Mexico

ROLE Founder and former leader of Amazon

ACCOMPLISHMENTS

Started Amazon and grew it into one of the world's largest retailers

In 1998, Amazon began selling CDs and DVDs. The next year, Amazon added toys and video games. Photography items were added in 2000.

TIME-HONORED

In 1999, *Time* magazine named Jeff its Person of the Year. This was for his role in making online shopping more popular.

AMAZON.COM IN 1999

AMAZON FULFILLMENT CENTER IN GERMANY IN 1999

JEFF WITH THIRD-PARTY PRODUCTS

Amazon grew in another way that year. It added sellers. In Amazon's early years, it was the site's only seller. In 2000, it introduced a **third-party marketplace**. The marketplace let small businesses and large **brands** sell items on Amazon. Amazon's popularity drew many buyers to the third-party marketplace. The sellers gave Amazon part of their earnings from sales they made on the site.

As Amazon grew, so did its **inventory**. It started to sell almost everything! In 2000, Amazon added an arrow to its **logo** to show this idea. The arrow pointed from the A to the Z in "Amazon." This showed that Amazon sold everything "from A to Z."

AMAZON PRODUCTS

2007	KINDLE
2011	AMAZON FIRE
2014	ECHO
2014	FIRE TV STICK
2017	ECHO SHOW
2021	BLINK VIDEO DOORBELL

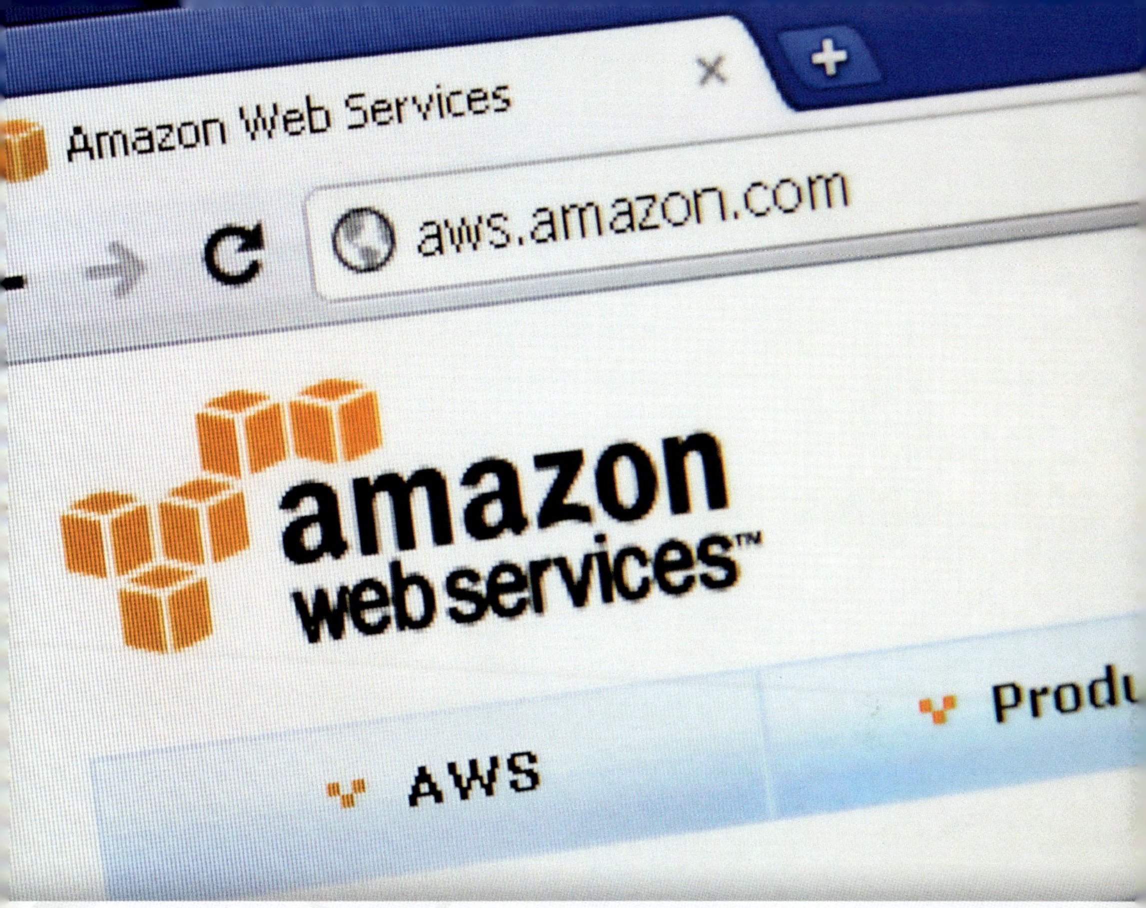

In 2002, Amazon started AWS. AWS offers **cloud computing** services to organizations and businesses. In 2023, AWS earned the company more than $90 billion. The service hosted more than 50 million websites!

SMILE
The arrow in Amazon's logo is curved. This is so it looks like a smile.

PRIME LOGO

Amazon's next big offering came in 2005 with Prime. Prime promised superfast shipping for a yearly fee. Millions of items were available on the service. Subscribers could receive them in only two days! The next year, Fulfillment by Amazon added even more items. Third-party marketplace sellers could use Amazon to ship more quickly!

In 2007, Amazon took another huge step with the Kindle e-reader. At launch, there were more than 90,000 e-books available. The first Kindle sold out within hours. Since its release, many new versions have been created!

LISTEN UP

Amazon bought Audible in 2008. Today, more than 50 million subscribers use Audible to listen to books, podcasts, and more!

2019 KINDLE PAPERWHITE

EARLY KINDLE E-READER

ALWAYS GROWING

AMAZON BASICS PRODUCTS

Amazon continued to add its own products. In 2009, the company introduced Amazon Basics. It started as a brand of electronics. It sold cables and other **accessories**. Today, Amazon Basics includes many household goods.

Many other Amazon brands have been added. Amazon Essentials offers clothing and accessories. Amazon Elements sells health items such as baby supplies and vitamins. Wickedly Prime is Amazon's brand of snacks. By 2020, Amazon shoppers could find more than 240,000 Amazon-branded products on the site!

POPULAR AMAZON BRANDS

AMAZON BASICS
What It Sells: household goods

AMAZON ESSENTIALS
What It Sells: clothing and accessories

AMAZON ELEMENTS
What It Sells: health items

WAG
What It Sells: dog food

WICKEDLY PRIME
What It Sells: snack foods

Amazon also continued to add more services. In 2011, Amazon added TV shows and movies for Prime subscribers. By 2023, Prime Video included more than 2,700 TV shows. It had over 26,000 movies!

In 2013, Amazon **Studios** began releasing its own original TV shows. Many of Amazon's original shows are for kids. These include *Just Add Magic* and *Creative Galaxy*. Amazon also makes popular movies. Some of its shows and movies have even won awards!

JUST ADD MAGIC CAST

AMAZON TIMELINE

1994 — Jeff Bezos starts Amazon.com to sell books

1998 — Amazon begins selling CDs and DVDs

1997 — One-click ordering is added to Amazon

1999 — Amazon begins selling toys, tools, video games, and more

2000 — Amazon introduces a third-party marketplace

2002 — AWS is launched

2005 — Amazon Prime is first offered

2007 — The Kindle e-reader is released

2009 — The Amazon Basics brand launches

2011 — Amazon Prime subscribers can stream TV shows and movies

2014 — Alexa is introduced

2023 — Amazon tests delivering packages using a new drone

STUDIO SHAKE-UP

In 2022, Amazon bought the film company MGM. Two years later, Amazon Studios changed its name. It became Amazon MGM Studios.

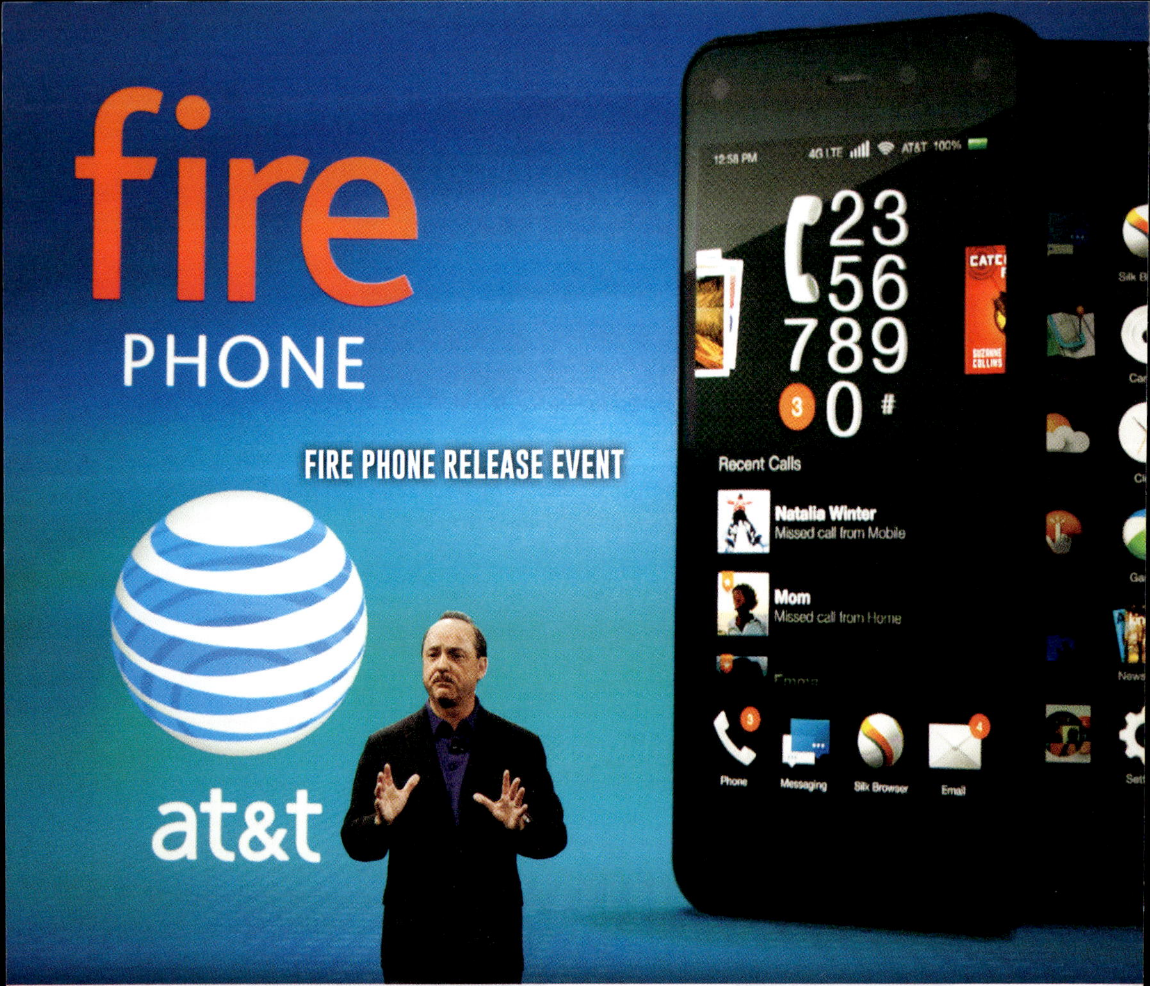

FIRE PHONE RELEASE EVENT

In 2014, Amazon introduced its next big electronic product. That June, the Amazon Fire smartphone came out. Amazon hoped it would be very popular. But the phone was costly. People did not like its features. It was not successful.

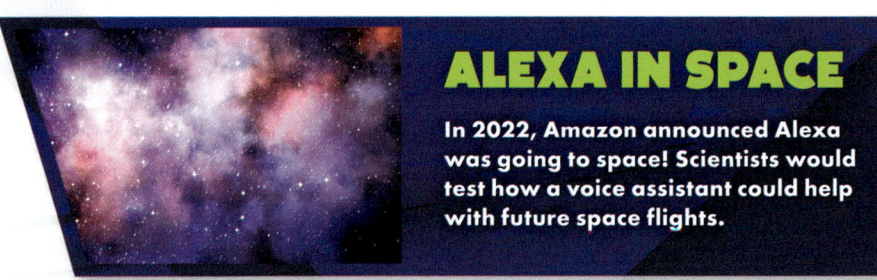

ALEXA IN SPACE

In 2022, Amazon announced Alexa was going to space! Scientists would test how a voice assistant could help with future space flights.

Later that year, Amazon released the Echo smart speaker. It was made to use with the Alexa **voice assistant**. People could tell Alexa to order products and play music. Alexa helped make the Echo a hit. Today, many different versions have been released!

AMAZON EARNINGS

Amazon has grown its business in other ways, too. In 2014, the company bought Twitch, a popular live-streaming service. In 2017, Amazon bought the Whole Foods Market grocery store chain.

TWITCH APP

WHOLE FOODS MARKET

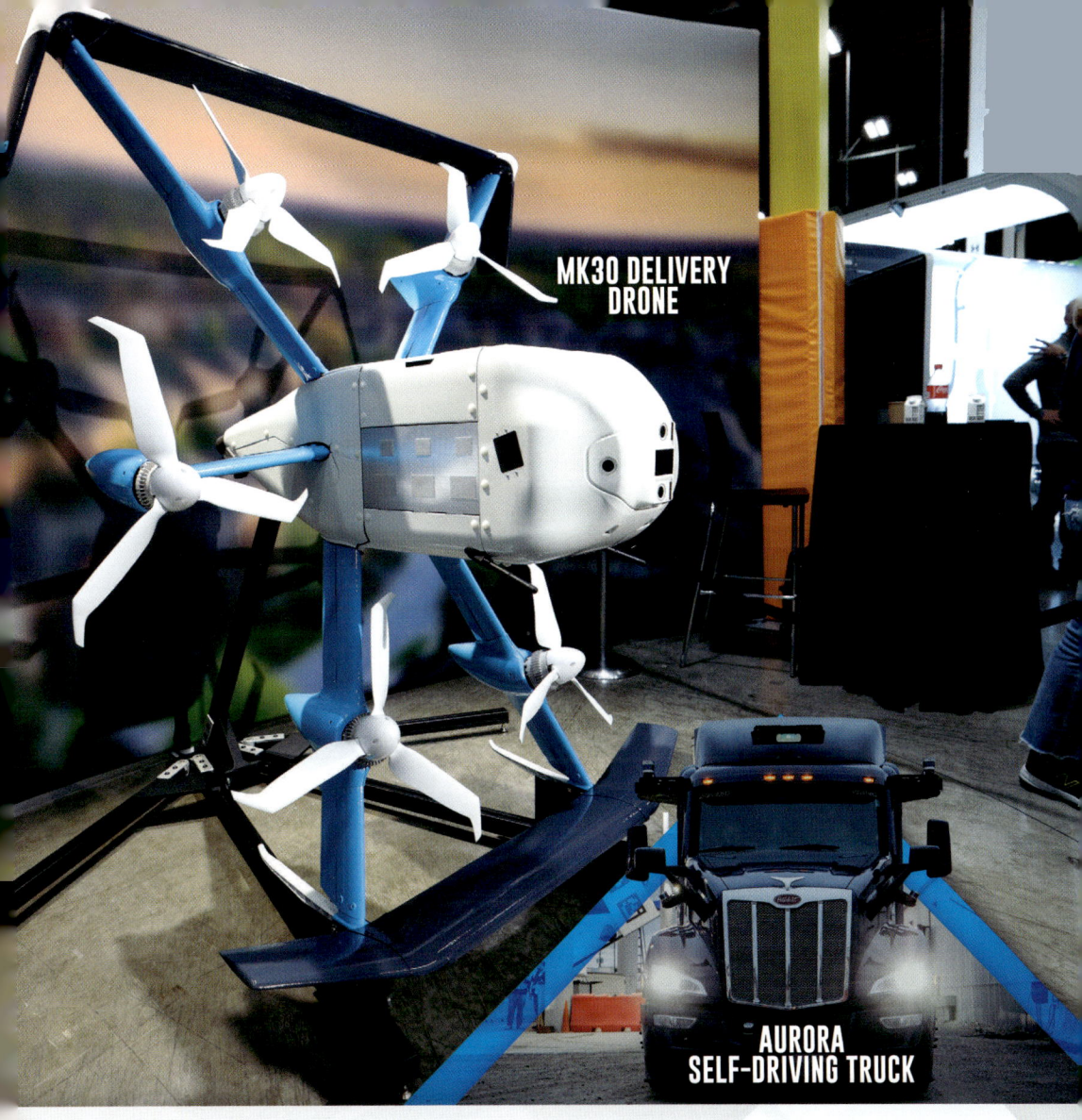

MK30 DELIVERY DRONE

AURORA SELF-DRIVING TRUCK

Two years later, Amazon bought part of Aurora, a self-driving car company. Aurora plans to make self-driving cars safer and faster. This could help Amazon make deliveries even more quickly! In 2024, Amazon tested new **drones** for package delivery. In the future, Amazon could expand to sell houses or offer banking services. The sky is the limit for this ruling retailer!

HELPING OTHERS

2019 AMAZON FUTURE ENGINEER STUDENTS

Amazon supports many important causes. Fulfillment by Amazon gives 50,000 items to people in need every day! Amazon also gives money through special programs. Amazon Future Engineer is one. In 2022, this program gave a total of $16 million to 400 students for use in science education.

Amazon also helps people access food and housing. In 2022, it gave over $12 million to feed people in need. The company's Housing **Equity** Fund has provided more than $2 billion to help people access affordable housing. The company also provides technology training and help to people affected by disasters.

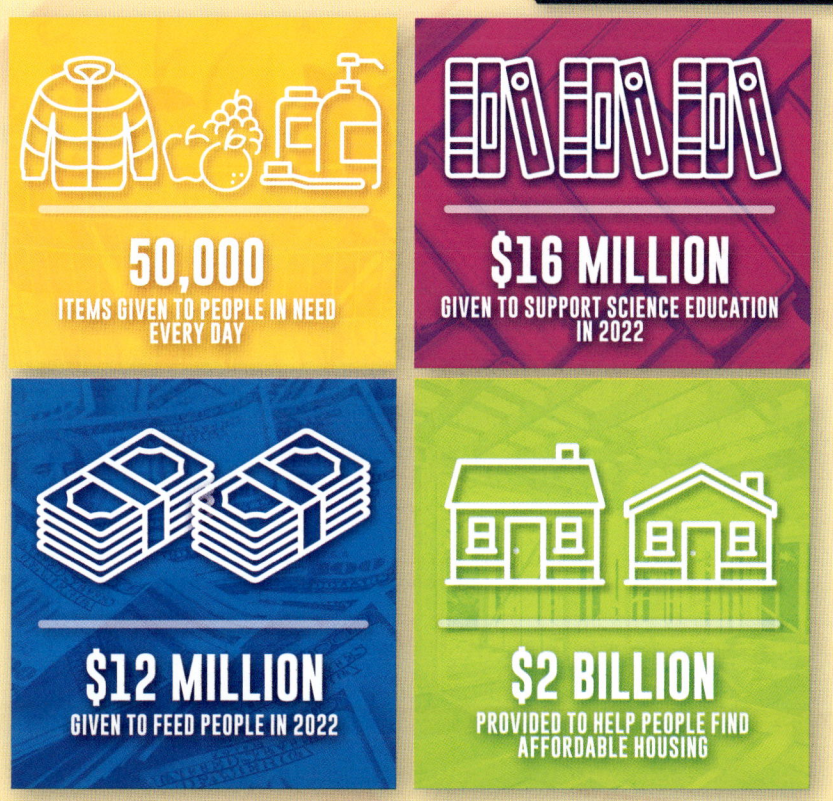

GIVING BACK

50,000
ITEMS GIVEN TO PEOPLE IN NEED EVERY DAY

$16 MILLION
GIVEN TO SUPPORT SCIENCE EDUCATION IN 2022

$12 MILLION
GIVEN TO FEED PEOPLE IN 2022

$2 BILLION
PROVIDED TO HELP PEOPLE FIND AFFORDABLE HOUSING

A SPECIAL HOLIDAY

PRIME DAY POSTER AT WHOLE FOODS MARKET

People love to shop on Amazon. The brand even has its own holiday! Prime Day is a global event. It usually lasts two days once or twice a year. Prime subscribers get discounts on many items. In 2023, Prime Day shoppers bought more than 375 million items! Sales on the first day reached a company record $6.4 billion!

28

Amazon changed the way people shop. Now, people expect fast shipping on millions of items on Amazon. Amazon shows no sign of slowing down. It continues to offer new services, entertainment, products, and more!

PRIME DAY

WHAT IT IS
A holiday for Amazon Prime subscribers

WHERE IT IS
Amazon's website and app

WHEN IT IS
Two days once or twice a year

ACTIVITIES
Prime subscribers shop for deals on Amazon items

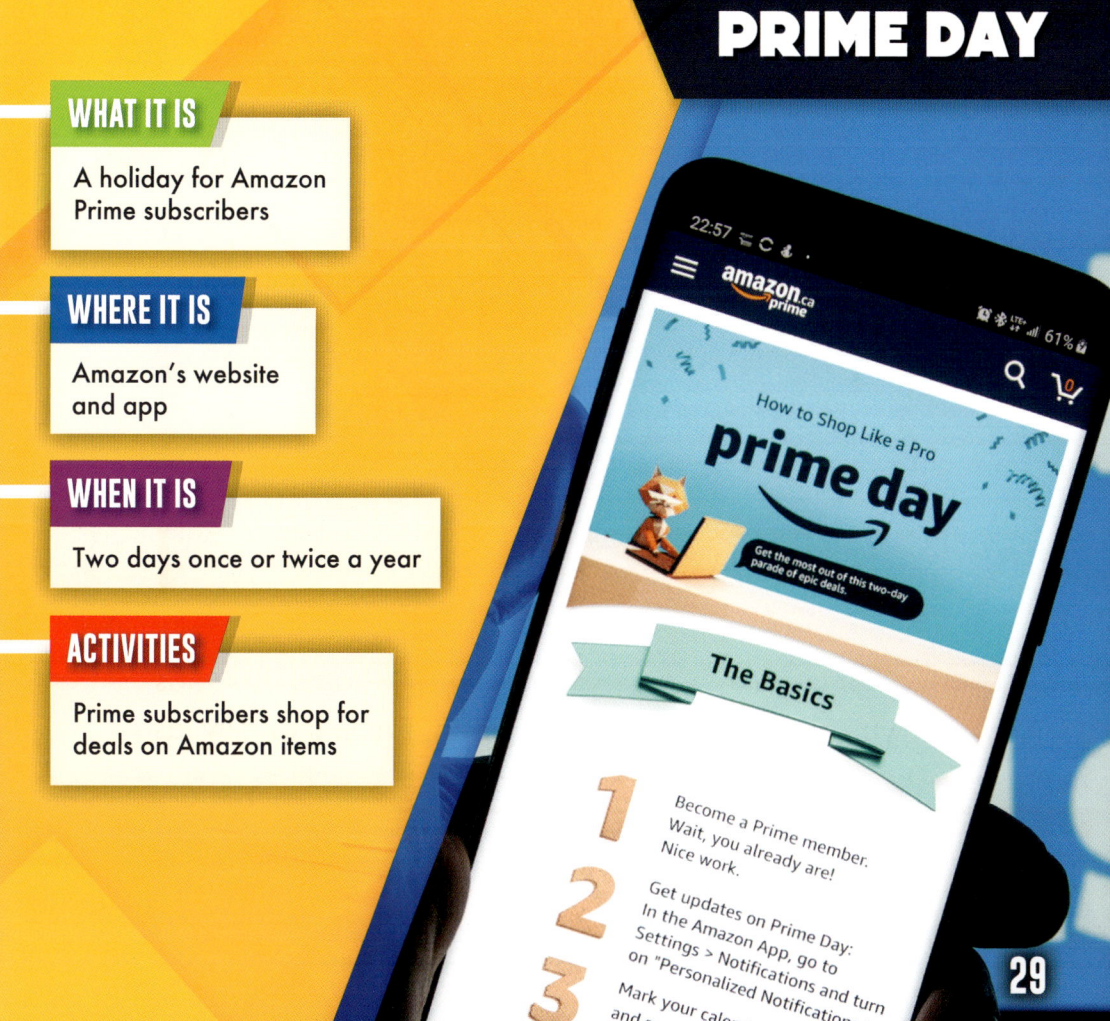

GLOSSARY

accessories—items added to something else to make it more useful or attractive

app—a program such as a game or internet browser; an app is also called an application.

brands—categories of products all made by the same company

cloud computing—technology that allows people to store, save, and use data on the internet instead of on individual computers

drones—aircraft flown by a remote control or a computer

equity—making something fair based on people's needs

fulfillment centers—places where orders are packed and shipped

headquarters—a company's main office

inventory—a full list of items or goods

logo—a symbol or design that identifies a brand or product

retailers—sellers of goods

studios—places where movies are filmed

subscribers—people who sign up for something in order to get easy access to its content

subsidiaries—companies owned or controlled by another, larger company

third-party marketplace—a marketplace owned by one company that sells products for other companies

voice assistant—software that responds to voice commands to do tasks

TO LEARN MORE

AT THE LIBRARY

Duling, Kaitlyn. *How the Internet Changed the World.* New York, N.Y.: Cavendish Square, 2019.

Furgang, Adam. *Jeff Bezos: Tech Entrepreneur and Businessman.* New York, N.Y.: Enslow Publishing, 2019.

Goldstein, Margaret J. *The Genius of Amazon: How Jeff Bezos and Online Shopping Changed the World.* Minneapolis, Minn.: Lerner Publications, 2023.

ON THE WEB

FACTSURFER

Factsurfer.com gives you a safe, fun way to find more information.

1. Go to www.factsurfer.com.

2. Enter "Amazon" into the search box and click 🔍.

3. Select your book cover to see a list of related content.

INDEX

Alexa, 22, 23
Amazon Future Engineer, 26
Amazon products, 14
Amazon Studios, 20, 21
Amazon Web Services, 7, 15
app, 5, 24
Arlington, Virginia, 6, 7
Audible, 17
Aurora, 25
Bellevue, Washington, 9
Bezos, Jeff, 8, 9, 11, 12, 13
books, 8, 9, 10, 17
brands, 13, 18, 19, 28
drones, 25
earnings, 23
Echo, 7, 23
Fulfillment by Amazon, 16, 26
fulfillment centers, 7, 10, 12
giving back, 27
Housing Equity Fund, 27
Kindle, 7, 17

logo, 14, 15, 16
name, 9
one-click ordering, 10, 11
popular Amazon brands, 19
Prime, 16, 20, 28
Prime Day, 28, 29
Prime Video, 7, 20
products, 5, 7, 8, 9, 10, 12, 13, 14, 16, 17, 18, 19, 22, 23, 28, 29
sales, 11, 13, 15, 28
Seattle, Washington, 6, 7
smartphone, 5, 22
subscribers, 7, 16, 17, 20, 28
third-party marketplace, 13, 16
timeline, 21
Twitch, 7, 24
Whole Foods Market, 7, 24, 28

The images in this book are reproduced through the courtesy of: CHUYN, front cover (delivery truck); Jonathan Weiss, front cover (Amazon packages); AjayTvm, front cover (Echo Dot); BigTunaOnline, front cover (Amazon app); Picturesque Japan, front cover (Fire TV stick); Lets Design Studio, front cover (Amazon Go); VDB Photos, front cover (Echo Look); Cineberg, front cover (Prime delivery agent); CL Shebley, front cover (Prime robot); Shutterstock, front cover (logo); Birgit Reitz-Hofmann, p. 2; Ian Dewar Photography, p. 3; StockImageFactory, pp. 4-5; Hadrian, p. 5 (packaging); Framesira, p. 5 (iPhone); Francis Specker/ Alamy, p. 6 (Amazon Go store); CK Foto, p. 6 (Amazon headquarters); SCStock, p. 7 (Seattle, Washington); WorldFoto/ Alamy, p. 8; Cascade Creatives, p. 9 (Bellevue, Washington); worldclassphoto, p. 9 (Amazon River); Sundry Photography, p. 9 (Get Big Fast); ASSOCIATED PRESS/ AP Newsroom, p. 10; Geekwire, p. 10 (shopping buttons); dpa picture alliance archive, p. 11 (Jeff Bezos); skodonnell, p. 11 (Amazon boxes); Tom Bible/ Alamy, p. 12 (Jeff Bezos); Patti McConville, p. 12 (Amazon webpage); picture alliance/ Getty Images, p. 12; Chris Carroll/ Getty Images, p. 13; NotFromUtrecht/ Wikipedia, p. 14 (Kindle); pixelfit, p. 14 (Amazon Fire); Frmorrison/ Wikipedia, p. 14 (Echo); urbanbuzz, p. 14 (Fire TV stick); MOTOSHI, p. 14 (Echo Show); Jamie McCarthy/ Getty Images, p. 14 (Blink Video doorbell); Web Pix/ Alamy, p. 15; Sanur Karib, p. 15 (logo); Bloomberg/ Getty Images, pp. 16, 18, 25 (Aurora); Claudio Divizia, p. 16 (Prime logo); Ralf Liebhold, p. 17 (Audible); Muhammad Fadhli Adnan, p. 18 (Kindle Paperwhite); Barry Mason/ Alamy, p. 17 (early Kindle); Sergio Yoneda, p. 19 (Amazon Basics); Todd Williamson/ Getty Images, p. 20 (Just Add Magic cast); rawf8, p. 20 (Prime Video); Artur Marfin, p. 21 (DVDs); Konektus Photo, p. 21 (1999 toy); Ken Wolter, p. 21 (Amazon Basics); Joni Hanebutt, p. 21 (Alexa); chrisdorney, p. 21 (MGM logo); David Ryder/ Getty Images, p. 22; A MUSTAFA, p. 22 (space); Kits Pix, p. 23 (Amazon envelope); dennizn, pp. 23 (Amazon gift card), 29; Bilanol, p. 23 (Amazon box); XanderSt, p. 24 (Twitch app); Trong Nguyen, p. 24 (Whole Foods Market); JASON REDMOND/ Getty Images, p. 25 (MK30 delivery drone); Paras Griffin/ Getty Images, p. 26; New Africa, p. 27 (feature top left); Iren Moroz, p. 27 (feature top right); ElenaR, p. 27 (feature bottom left); anatoliy_gleb, p. 27 (feature bottom right); Sundry Photography/ Alamy, p. 28; dean bertoncelj, p. 31 (Kindle); Matt Gush, p. 31 (delivery truck).